Low Point

spice

over 60 recipes low in Points

SIMON & SCHUSTER
A VIACOM COMPANY

Joy Skipper

First published in Great Britain by Simon & Schuster UK Ltd, 2003
A Viacom Company

© Weight Watchers International Inc. 2003. All rights reserved.
No part of this publication may be reproduced, stored or
transmitted in any form or by any means without the prior
permission of Weight Watchers (UK) Ltd. Weight Watchers®,
Points® and **Time To Eat**™ are trademarks of Weight Watchers
International Inc. and used under its control by Weight
Watchers (UK) Ltd.

Simon & Schuster UK Ltd
Africa House
64–78 Kingsway
London
WC2B 6AH

Photography by Iain Bagwell
Styling by Marian Price
Food preparation by Penny Stephens

Design by Jane Humphrey
Typesetting by Stylize Digital Artwork
Printed and bound in China

Weight Watchers Publications Manager: Corrina Griffin
Weight Watchers Publications Executives: Lucy Davidson,
Mandy Spittle
Weight Watchers Publications Assistant: Nina Bhogal

A CIP catalogue for this book is available from the British Library

ISBN 0 74323 903 2

Pictured on the front cover: Fish Stew with Saffron, page 53

Pictured on the back cover: Chicken Jalfrezi, page 24

Raw Eggs: Only the freshest eggs should be used. Pregnant
women, the elderly and children should avoid recipes with
eggs which are not fully cooked or raw.

All fruits, vegetables and eggs are medium size unless otherwise
stated.

Recipe timings are approximate and meant to be guidelines.
Please note that the preparation time includes all the steps
up to and following the main cooking time(s).

 You'll find this easy to read logo on every recipe
throughout the book. The logo represents the
number of Points per serving each recipe contains.
The easy to use Points system is designed to help
you eat what you want, when you want – as long
as you stay within your Points allowance – giving
you the freedom to enjoy the food you love.

(V) This symbol denotes a vegetarian recipe and
assumes vegetarian cheese and free range eggs
are used. Virtually fat free fromage frais and low
fat crème fraîche may contain traces of gelatine
so they are not always vegetarian: please check
the labels.

(Vg) This symbol denotes a vegan dish.

contents

spice 'n' easy

low Point dishes

Welcome to *Low Point Spice*, the cookbook that shows you how to enjoy your favourite hot and spicy dishes the easy, low Point way. Gone are the traditional dieting days when curries and stir fries were off the menu – with Weight Watchers you *can* enjoy delicious, satisfying food and still be healthy and slim. With so many exotic herbs and spices now readily available, it is so easy to create these fantastic dishes from far flung countries – curries from Thailand, bhajis from India and even a cheesecake from Russia!

There's a great selection of hot and spicy dishes here. You'll find all the traditional favourites, like chicken korma and sweet and sour prawns, for just a fraction of the traditional Points! There's also a wonderful variety of newer, more exotic dishes like saffron chicken with apricots and vegetarian jungle curry where the delicate flavours will stir up your senses! There are meals for one or two, delicious vegetarian dishes, along with the traditional meat, fish and poultry options, making sure that there is something for everyone. You'll also find some fantastic starters to fire up your taste-buds and some cooling desserts to take off the heat from your meal!

Many of us, these days, have busy lifestyles, and Weight Watchers understands that there simply isn't the time to spend hours in the kitchen creating the perfect meal! So, for the recipes in this book, simplicity is the key. Even the recipes that look wonderfully impressive are easy to prepare and have step by step instructions, ensuring that nothing is too complicated! And even though the ingredients may be exotic, they are all widely available in most supermarkets.

Taste is the measure of a recipe's success, and the amount of spice specified in the recipe is just a guideline – so be bold and trust your taste-buds! If you like your food hotter or milder, just adjust the amount of spice according to your taste. Variety is the spice of life, and there are lots of fantastic flavours here to experiment with and some wonderful variations with most of the recipes. That's the joy of Weight Watchers and Time To Eat – simple, fantastic and tasty food – just the way *you* like it!

snacks and starters

This chapter gives you a delightful variety of wonderful snacks and starters, with something to suit every occasion. You'll find warming soups, which are ideal for a cold winter's day, and tasty dips and nibbles that are perfect for a summer garden party. There are also some lovely light lunches and delicious dinner party starters. All the recipes are low in Points, easy to prepare and taste fantastic – helping you to enjoy the food you love.

SESAME PRAWN TOASTS

14 Points per recipe
Makes 12
Preparation time: 25 minutes
Cooking time: 6–8 minutes
Calories per serving: 75
Freezing: not recommended

A delicious low Point version of this popular starter.

1 small (150 g/5½ oz) French stick, cut into 1 cm (½ inch) thick slices
80 g (3 oz) shelled prawns
80 g (3 oz) pork mince
1 spring onion, sliced finely
1 garlic clove, crushed
1 egg, beaten
½ teaspoon fish sauce (nam pla)
1 tablespoon chopped fresh coriander
2 tablespoons sesame seeds
2 tablespoons sweet chilli sauce
salt and freshly ground black pepper

1 Toast the French stick slices on one side and set aside.
2 Place the prawns in a blender and blend until nearly smooth. Add the pork and blend together with the prawns.
3 Place the prawn and pork mixture in a bowl and add the other ingredients, apart from the sesame seeds and chilli sauce. Season and mix well.
4 Heat a small frying pan and cook the prawn mixture for 3–4 minutes, stirring constantly.
5 Preheat the grill and spoon the mixture on to the untoasted side of the bread– press down well and then sprinkle with sesame seeds.
6 Grill for 3–4 minutes, until the sesame seeds start to turn golden. Serve with chilli sauce.

Top tip When buying fresh coriander, choose deep green leaves – these will be the freshest and tastiest.

Sesame Prawn
Toasts: A tasty
starter for just
1 Point per
serving.

**Spicy Nuts:
Perfect for the
party season
and only 3½
Points per
serving.**

SPICY NUTS

27½ Points per recipe

 Serves 8

Preparation time: 5 minutes

Cooking time: 15 minutes

Calories per serving: 205

Freezing: not recommended

Delicious to nibble with a pre-dinner drink and much more impressive than opening a packet!

1 teaspoon salt

¼ teaspoon artificial sweetener

½ teaspoon ground ginger

½ teaspoon ground coriander

½ teaspoon ground cinnamon

½ teaspoon ground cumin

½ teaspoon garam masala

100 g (3½ oz) cashew nuts

100 g (3½ oz) pecan nuts

50 g (1¾ oz) almonds

low fat cooking spray

1 Preheat the oven to Gas Mark 6/200°C/fan oven 180°C.

2 Mix together the salt, sweetener and all the spices. Add 1 tablespoon of water to make a paste.

3 Mix the nuts together in a bowl and add the paste. Mix really well to coat the nuts in the paste.

4 Spray a roasting tray with low fat cooking spray and pour in the nuts.

5 Cook in the oven for 10 minutes. Stir the nuts and then cook for a further 5 minutes. Remove from the oven and allow to cool in the tin.

Top tip These nuts will keep for a few days if stored in an airtight container.

Variation Any combination of nuts work well in this recipe – try peanuts and brazil nuts instead of the cashew and pecan nuts. The Points per serving will remain the same.

GUACAMOLE

8 Points per recipe

 Serves 2

Preparation time: 10 minutes

Calories per serving: 105

Freezing: not recommended

A great way to serve avocados – the spicy Mexican way!

1 medium avocado pear, stone removed

1 teaspoon lemon or lime juice

½ garlic clove, crushed

1 plum tomato, chopped

1 spring onion, sliced finely

a pinch of chilli powder

1 tablespoon chopped fresh coriander

salt and freshly ground black pepper

1 medium pitta bread, to serve

1 Scoop the flesh from the avocado into a bowl and mash with the lemon or lime juice.

2 Add the remaining ingredients, except the pitta, and mix together well.

3 Toast and slice the pitta bread, and serve with the guacamole.

Top tip Avocados turn brown if left for too long when out of their skins, so mash with lemon or lime juice as soon as you have scooped out the flesh.

Variation For a lower Point version of this dish, omit the pitta and replace with No Point crudités of your choice (e.g. carrots and celery). The Points will be reduced to 3 per serving.

Guacamole: The sunny flavours of Mexico for 4 Points per serving.

CURRIED PARSNIP SOUP

 1 POINT

4 Points per recipe

ⓋⓋⓖ *Serves 4*

Preparation time: 15 minutes
Cooking time: 18–20 minutes
Calories per serving: 65
Freezing: recommended for up to 1 month

Nothing beats a home made, warming soup, perfect to perk you up on a cold winter's day.

low fat cooking spray
1 onion, chopped
400 g (14 oz) parsnips, peeled and chopped
1 teaspoon curry powder
1 teaspoon ground ginger
1 teaspoon ground cumin
850 ml (1½ pints) vegetable stock
salt and freshly ground black pepper

1 Spray a medium saucepan with low fat cooking spray and sauté the onion for 4–5 minutes until beginning to soften.
2 Add the parsnips and spices and stir well to coat the vegetables with the spices.
3 Pour in the stock, season, bring to the boil and then simmer for 18–20 minutes, until the parsnips are tender.
4 Take off the heat and leave to cool for a couple of minutes.
5 When slightly cooled, blend the soup with a hand blender or in a food processor.
6 Check the seasoning, reheat and serve.

Variation For a No Point alternative, try curried cauliflower soup. Just substitute a medium cauliflower for the parsnips and follow the method above.

ROASTED AUBERGINE DIP

 0 POINTS

0 Points per recipe

ⓋⓋⓖ *Serves 2*

Preparation time: 8 minutes
Cooking time: 30 minutes
Calories per serving: 35
Freezing: not recommended

Try this dip for a change – it's so easy to make, tastes wonderful and yet, unbelievably it's No Points!

1 large aubergine
1 teaspoon soy sauce
1 teaspoon sweet chilli sauce
½ teaspoon lemon juice
1 tablespoon chopped fresh coriander
2 spring onions, sliced finely
No Point crudités, e.g. carrots and celery, to serve

1 Preheat the oven to Gas Mark 6/ 200°C/fan oven 180°C.
2 Cut the aubergine in half lengthways and score the flesh with a sharp knife. Place in the oven on a baking sheet and cook for 30 minutes.
3 Leave to cool and then scrape away the flesh from the skin. Discard the skin.
4 Place the flesh in a food processor with the soy sauce, chilli sauce and lemon juice. Blitz until smooth.
5 Mix in the chopped fresh coriander and sliced spring onions and serve with the No Point crudités.

SPICY POTATOES

 2 POINTS

9 Points per recipe

ⓋⓋⓖ *Serves 4*

Preparation time: 8 minutes
Cooking time: 25–30 minutes
Calories per serving: 165
Freezing: not recommended
Points per serving:

A delicious way of serving potatoes, with fresh tomatoes and lots of spice.

½ teaspoon mustard seeds
½ teaspoon cumin seeds
4 medium potatoes (600g/1 lb 5 oz) , peeled and chopped
½ teaspoon cayenne pepper
½ teaspoon turmeric
½ teaspoon freshly grated ginger
2 tablespoons ground coriander
4 tomatoes, chopped
1 tablespoon desiccated coconut
salt

1 Place the mustard and cumin seeds in a medium pan over a medium heat.
2 When they start to 'pop' add the potatoes, cayenne pepper, turmeric, ginger and coriander. Mix really well to coat the potatoes in the spices.
3 Add 100 ml (3½ fl oz) of water, stir gently and bring to a simmer. Cover and simmer for 15 minutes.
4 Add the tomatoes, coconut and salt and stir well. Cover again and cook for another 10–15 minutes until the potatoes are tender, then serve.

Spicy Potatoes: A lively accompaniment for just 2 Points per serving.

Sweetcorn and Crab Soup: A light and tasty soup for just 2 Points per serving.

SWEETCORN AND CRAB SOUP

7½ Points per recipe

Serves 4
Preparation time: 5 minutes
Cooking time: 10 minutes
Calories per serving: 135
Freezing: not recommended

A delicious soup filled with sweetcorn and crab – great as a starter or even a light lunch.

1 egg white
1 teaspoon sesame oil
1.2 litres (2 pints) chicken stock
275 g (9½ oz) canned or frozen sweetcorn
1 tablespoon soy sauce
2 teaspoons chopped fresh root ginger
2 teaspoons cornflour, mixed with 2 teaspoons water
225 g (8 oz) canned crabmeat
4 spring onions, chopped
freshly ground black pepper

1 Beat the egg white and sesame oil together and leave to one side.
2 Bring the stock to the boil in a large pan and add the sweetcorn. Simmer for 5 minutes and then add the soy sauce, ginger, pepper and cornflour paste.
3 Bring back to the boil, lower the heat to a simmer and add the crabmeat.
4 Slowly pour in the egg white and sesame oil mixture, stirring constantly.
5 Sprinkle over the spring onions and serve.

Top tip When buying fresh ginger, always select firm, unshrivelled pieces and peel off the skin before use.

Variation Chicken and sweetcorn soup can be made in the same way – substitute the same amount of cooked shredded chicken for the crab meat. The Points per serving will be 2½.

ALOO GOBI

5 Points per recipe

 Serves 4
Preparation time: 10 minutes
Cooking time: 30 minutes
Calories per serving: 135
Freezing: not recommended

Spice up your vegetables with this easy but tasty vegetable dish 'Aloo' means potato and 'gobi' means cauliflower.

low fat cooking spray
3 onions, chopped
1 medium cauliflower, cut into florets
3 medium potatoes, peeled and chopped
2 teaspoons grated fresh ginger
2 tomatoes, chopped
¼ teaspoon cayenne pepper
½ teaspoon turmeric
1½ teaspoons ground coriander
1½ teaspoons salt
½ teaspoon garam masala
½ teaspoon cumin seeds

1 Spray a large saucepan with low fat cooking spray and sauté the onions for 3–4 minutes until beginning to soften.
2 Add the cauliflower florets, potatoes, ginger, tomatoes, cayenne pepper, turmeric, ground coriander and salt and mix really well to coat the vegetables in the spices.
3 Pour in 100 ml (3½ fl oz) of water, bring to a simmer and then cover and simmer gently for 15 minutes.
4 Add the garam masala and cumin seeds, mix well and then cover again and cook for a further 15 minutes until the potatoes are tender. Serve hot.

Top tip The heat in this recipe comes from the cayenne pepper, so just adjust the amount you use, according to how hot you like your food.

Variation For an even more substantial dish add a drained 410 g can of chick peas at step 4 with the garam masala and cumin. The Points will then be 3 per serving.

SPICY CHICK PEA AND LENTIL SOUP

17 Points per recipe

Ⓥ Ⓥᴱ Serves 6

Preparation time: 15 minutes

Cooking time: 15–20 minutes

Calories per serving: 165

Freezing: recommended for up to 1 month

A thick, warming and filling soup, with lots of nutritional goodness. Perfect for a chilly autumnal day.

low fat cooking spray
1 red onion, diced
2 celery sticks, diced
2 carrots, diced
1 garlic clove, crushed
50 g (1³/₄ oz) Puy lentils
50 g (1³/₄ oz) red split lentils
1 teaspoon ground cumin
¹/₂ teaspoon ground coriander
1 teaspoon grated fresh root ginger
400 g can chopped tomatoes
410 g can chick peas, drained
850 ml (1¹/₂ pints) vegetable stock
200 ml (7 fl oz) reduced fat coconut milk
salt and freshly ground black pepper

1 Spray a large saucepan with low fat cooking spray. Add the onion, celery, carrots and garlic and cook for 2–3 minutes.

2 Add the lentils and then the spices and stir well to coat the vegetables.

3 Add the chopped tomatoes and chick peas and pour in the stock. Bring to the boil and simmer for 15 minutes.

4 Pour in the coconut milk and stir well.

5 Pour a third of the soup into a food processor or liquidiser and blend very briefly to retain some of the chunkiness of the vegetables.

6 Return the blended soup to the pan. Stir, reheat, check the seasoning and serve.

Variation For a non vegetarian version, add 50 g (1³/₄ oz) lean back bacon when frying the vegetables. The Points will then be 3¹/₂ per serving.

THAI PRAWN PARCELS

10¹/₂ Points per recipe

Makes 10

Preparation time: 20 minutes

Cooking time: 15 minutes

Calories per parcel: 60

Freezing: not recommended

These parcels are a delicious, savoury treat. They're really easy to do and only 1 point each!

200 g (7 oz) prawns
2 tablespoons freshly chopped coriander
125 g (4¹/₂ oz) filo pastry
1 tablespoon red Thai curry paste
low fat cooking spray
salt and freshly ground black pepper

1 Place the prawns, coriander and seasoning in a blender or food processor and blend briefly until coarsely chopped. Preheat the oven to Gas Mark 6/200°C/fan oven 180°C.

2 Cut the pastry into squares measuring roughly 10–13 cm (4–5 inches); you need 30 squares in total. Place one square on a board and spray with low fat cooking spray. Spray two more squares and stack them on top of the first square.

3 Spread a small amount of Thai paste over the centre of the pastry and then top with about 1 tablespoon of the prawn mixture. Bring the sides of the pastry up and pinch together.

4 Spray with a little low fat cooking spray and place on a baking sheet.

5 Repeat with the remaining pastry and prawn mixture. Bake in the oven for 15 minutes until golden.

CHICKEN SATAY

9 Points per recipe

Serves 4

Preparation time: 15 minutes + 1 hour marinating

Cooking time: 10–12 minutes

Calories per serving: 140

Freezing: not recommended

A deliciously nutty and spicy chicken dish – great for summer barbecues.

200 g (7 oz) skinless, boneless chicken breast, thinly sliced

For the marinade

½ tablespoon ground cinnamon

½ tablespoon ground cumin

freshly ground black pepper

50 ml (2 fl oz) soy sauce

For the satay sauce

1 teaspoon Thai green curry paste

2 tablespoons reduced fat coconut milk

2 tablespoons water

½ tablespoon muscovado sugar

40 g (1½ oz) peanuts, chopped finely

1 Mix together the marinade ingredients in a non metallic bowl. Place the strips of chicken meat in the marinade, cover with cling film and leave to marinate for at least 1 hour. Light the barbecue, if using, or preheat the grill to hot.

2 Thread the chicken strips on to 8 kebab skewers and pour over the remaining marinade.

3 In a small saucepan mix together the satay sauce ingredients. Bring to a simmer and continue to simmer until thickened – this takes about 2 minutes.

4 Meanwhile, place the chicken sticks on the barbecue or under a hot grill and cook for 10–12 minutes, turning occasionally until the chicken is cooked.

5 Serve the chicken sticks with the satay sauce poured over the chicken or in a side dish, ready to dip the chicken into.

Top tip If you are using wooden kebab sticks always soak them in cold water for 30 minutes before

using them. This will prevent them from burning when cooked under a grill or on a barbecue.

Variation Prawns are also great served this way. Use 200 g (7 oz) prawns instead of the chicken – the Points will remain the same.

Chicken Satay:
Only 2 Points
for 2 delicious
skewers.

ONION BHAJIS

5 Points per recipe

Ⓥ *Serves 4*

Preparation time: 10 minutes

Cooking time: 20 minutes

Calories per serving: 85

Freezing: not recommended

Everybody loves these – and they're even better home made! Serve with the lovely fresh cucumber raita for a cooling contrast.

1 onion, sliced thinly

¼ teaspoon coriander seeds, crushed

¼ teaspoon cumin seeds

4 tablespoons plain flour

a pinch of salt

low fat cooking spray

For the raita

100 g (3½ oz) low fat plain yogurt

½ cucumber, grated

a bunch of fresh mint, chopped

1 Place the onion, coriander and cumin seeds in a bowl and mix well. Sprinkle with the flour and salt. Mix again to coat the onion.

2 Add 2 tablespoons of water and mix until the onion is covered in a fine batter.

3 Heat a frying pan and spray with low fat cooking spray. Place individual tablespoonfuls of the onion mixture in the pan and press down to flatten slightly. Cook on each side for about 4–5 minutes until golden. Keep the bhajis warm, either in the oven or under a moderate grill, while you cook the remaining mixture. The mixture will make about 8 bhajis.

4 Mix together the ingredients for the raita and serve with the onion bhajis.

meals
for one or two

In this chapter you'll find lots of simple and delicious recipes to inspire you at those times when you are cooking for just one or two. The recipes are easy to prepare, full of flavour and have so few Points.

SPICY BEEF TACOS

6½ POINTS

13½ Points per recipe
Serves 2
Preparation time: 10 minutes
Cooking time: 25 minutes
Calories per serving: 410
Freezing: not recommended

A fun and filling Mexican dish – perfect for a midweek supper.

low fat cooking spray
1 onion, chopped
1 garlic clove, crushed
1 green pepper, de-seeded and chopped
1 red pepper, de-seeded and chopped
½ teaspoon cayenne pepper
200 g (7 oz) extra lean minced beef
1 tablespoon tomato purée
100 ml (3½ fl oz) water
4 taco shells
50 g (1¾ oz) half fat Cheddar cheese, grated
salt and freshly ground black pepper
No Point crisp green salad, to serve

1 Heat a frying pan and spray with low fat cooking spray. Add the onion, garlic and peppers and cook for 3–4 minutes, until starting to soften.

2 Sprinkle in the cayenne pepper and add the minced beef. Cook for 4–5 minutes, stirring occasionally, to brown all the meat.

3 Add the tomato purée, water and seasoning and bring to a simmer. Simmer for 12–15 minutes, until the liquid has been absorbed.

4 Heat the taco shells according to the instructions on the pack.

5 Spoon the spicy mince mixture into each taco shell. Sprinkle each one with grated cheese and serve with a crisp green No Point salad.

Top tip Taco shells can normally be found in most large supermarkets – look near the spicy canned and packet foods.

Variation Minced lamb, turkey or chicken could also be used for this recipe. The Points per serving will be 7½, 5½ and 5 respectively.

Spicy Beef Tacos: Seriously satisfying for 6½ Points per serving.

Tandoori Chicken:
A great British
favourite for
4 Points per
serving.

TANDOORI CHICKEN

8 Points per recipe

Serves 2
Preparation time: 25 minutes + marinating
Cooking time: 20–25 minutes
Calories per serving: 250
Freezing: not recommended

Tandoor is actually the name of the clay oven that is used to cook this dish, but it will taste just as good cooked in a normal oven!

2 medium skinless, boneless chicken breasts (165 g/5¾ oz), cut in half

½ teaspoon salt

1 tablespoon lemon juice

For the marinade

185 g (6½ oz) low fat plain yogurt

½ small onion, chopped

½ garlic clove, chopped

1 teaspoon peeled and chopped fresh root ginger

½ green chilli, de-seeded and chopped

1 teaspoon garam masala

For the raita

½ cucumber, grated

100 g (3½ oz) low fat plain yogurt

1 tablespoon chopped mint leaves

To serve

shredded iceberg lettuce

2 tomatoes, sliced

1 Make two slits in each of the four pieces of chicken. Lay the chicken pieces on a large plate. Sprinkle with half the salt and half the lemon juice and then turn the pieces over and repeat with the remaining salt and lemon juice. Leave to stand for 15 minutes.

2 Place all the marinade ingredients in a food processor or blender and blend until smooth.

3 Place the chicken and any leftover juices into a bowl and pour over the marinade. Rub the marinade into the slits of the chicken and then cover and leave to marinate for as long as you can – between 5–8 hours is ideal.

4 Preheat the oven to its hottest temperature and place a shelf near the top.

5 Spread the chicken pieces on a baking tray and bake for 20–25 minutes, until cooked through. The juices should run clear when the thickest part is pierced with a skewer.

6 Mix together the cucumber, yogurt and mint and serve with the chicken, along with shredded lettuce and sliced tomatoes.

Top tip Garam Masala is a mixture of ground spices that is used in Indian cookery. The term literally means 'hot spice'.

Variation Turkey breasts or pork fillets can be prepared in exactly the same way. The Points will then be 4 and 6 per serving respectively.

FALAFEL

6 Points per recipe

 Serves 2
Preparation time: 8 minutes
Cooking time: 10 minutes
Calories per serving: 205
Freezing: not recommended

A great little snack – perfect for taking on a picnic or for a packed lunch.

300 g (10½ oz) canned chick peas, drained

a small bunch of fresh coriander, chopped

½ teaspoon cumin seeds

¼ onion, grated

low fat cooking spray

50 g (1¾ oz) low fat yogurt

a small bunch of fresh mint, chopped

salt and freshly ground black pepper

To serve

crisp lettuce leaves

1 tablespoon each chopped coriander and parsley

1 Place the chick peas in a food processor or blender and blend until nearly smooth.

2 Transfer to a bowl and mix in the coriander, cumin seeds, grated onion and seasoning.

3 Shape into six little balls and then flatten out to make patties.

4 Heat a frying pan and spray with low fat cooking spray.

5 Place the falafel in the pan and cook for 4–5 minutes, until golden on one side. Then turn over and repeat for the other side.

6 Mix together the yogurt and mint.

7 Serve the falafel on a bed of crisp lettuce leaves and chopped coriander and parsley, with the yogurt drizzled over.

Thai Sweetcorn Fritters: Tasty little bites for 4 Points per serving.

THAI SWEETCORN FRITTERS WITH SALSA

4 POINTS

8 Points per recipe

Ⓥ Serves 2

Preparation time: 10 minutes

Cooking time: 20 minutes

Calories per serving: 265

Freezing: not recommended

A great snack for a summer lunch – delicately flavoured sweetcorn fritters with a spicy, refreshing salsa.

60 g (2 oz) plain flour
a pinch of chilli powder
a pinch of salt
1 small egg, beaten
80 ml (2³/₄ fl oz) reduced fat coconut milk
125 g (4¹/₂ oz) canned sweetcorn
2 spring onions, sliced
low fat cooking spray
salad leaves, to serve

For the salsa

¹/₂ red onion, diced
¹/₄ cucumber, diced
2 tomatoes, diced
1 tablespoon rice vinegar

1 Sift the flour, chilli powder and salt into a bowl and make a well in the centre.

2 Add the beaten egg and coconut milk and beat together to make a smooth batter. Add the sweetcorn and spring onions and mix well.

3 Spray a frying pan with low fat cooking spray and heat. Place individual tablespoonfuls of the sweetcorn batter into the pan and cook for 5–6 minutes. Then turn over and cook on the other side for 4–5 minutes, until golden. Remove from the pan and keep warm whilst cooking the remaining batter in the same way. The batter allows for 6 small or 4 medium fritters.

4 Mix the salsa ingredients together and serve with crunchy green salad leaves and the sweetcorn fritters.

Top tip Vinegars are widely used in Eastern cooking and, unlike Western vinegars, they are usually made from rice. If you cannot get rice vinegar substitute cider vinegar. The Points will remain the same.

SALMON AND THAI NOODLES

5 POINTS

10 Points per recipe

Serves 2

Preparation time: 6 minutes

Cooking time: 12–15 minutes

Calories per serving: 325

Freezing: not recommended

A mouthwatering noodle dish with spicy chunks of salmon and a tangy sweet chilli sauce.

60 g (2 oz) medium egg noodles
low fat cooking spray
1 garlic clove, crushed
1 teaspoon peeled and chopped fresh root ginger
¹/₂ lemon grass stalk, chopped finely
200 g (7 oz) salmon fillet, cut into bite size pieces
3 spring onions, chopped
3 teaspoons soy sauce
2 tablespoons sweet chilli sauce
2 tablespoons chopped fresh coriander
salt and freshly ground black pepper

1 Bring a pan of salted water to the boil and add the noodles. Simmer for 4 minutes and then drain.

2 Meanwhile, spray a frying pan or wok with low fat cooking spray and stir fry the garlic, ginger and lemon grass for 1–2 minutes.

3 Add the salmon and stir fry for another 4–5 minutes before adding the spring onions and soy sauce.

4 Add the sweet chilli sauce and 2 tablespoons of water. Simmer for 3–4 minutes before adding the egg noodles. Stir around to coat with the Thai sauce.

5 Check the seasoning, sprinkle with coriander and serve immediately.

Variation Use spaghetti or linguine instead of noodles. The Points remain the same.

Salmon and Thai Noodles: Deliciously fragrant for 5 Points per serving.

BRAISED SPICY BEANCURD

1 Point per recipe

Ⓥ Ⓥg Serves 1

Preparation time: 5 minutes

Cooking time: 8 minutes

Calories per serving: 105

Freezing: not recommended

A lively vegetarian dish with lots of flavour and hardly any Points.

25 g (1 oz) mange tout
40 g (1½ oz) baby sweetcorn
low fat cooking spray
60 g (2 oz) beancurd, cubed
½ green pepper, de-seeded and sliced
½ teaspoon peeled and chopped fresh root ginger
1 garlic clove, crushed
1 tablespoon yellow bean sauce

1 Steam the mange tout and baby sweetcorn for 6–8 minutes, until cooked but still crisp.

2 Meanwhile, heat a small frying pan and spray with low fat cooking spray. Put in the beancurd, green pepper, ginger and garlic. Stir fry for 3–4 minutes, until the beancurd is golden.

3 Add the yellow bean sauce and 3 tablespoons of water and stir whilst it bubbles and thickens.

4 Serve the beancurd with the steamed vegetables.

Variation This recipe can be used for spicy prawns – omit the beancurd and replace with 60 g (2 oz) of raw prawns. The Points will then be 1½ per serving.

Pasta Arrabbiata: A speedy and spicy meal for one – just 3½ Points.

PASTA ARRABBIATA

3½ POINTS

3½ Points per recipe

Ⓥ Serves 1

Preparation time: 5 minutes

Cooking time: 10 minutes

Calories per serving: 320

Freezing: not recommended

A pasta dish with a difference – it's hot and spicy! Perfect for a night on your own, as it takes no time at all.

60 g (2 oz) pasta shapes
low fat cooking spray
1 small onion, chopped
1 teaspoon chilli flakes
2 plum tomatoes, chopped
227 g canned chopped tomatoes
salt and freshly ground black pepper
1 teaspoon grated Parmesan, to serve

1 Bring a large pan of salted water to the boil and add the pasta. Cook according to the packet instructions (about 6–8 minutes).

2 Meanwhile, spray a small pan with low fat cooking spray and sauté the onion for 3–4 minutes. Add the chilli flakes, chopped fresh tomatoes and canned tomatoes. Simmer for 4–5 minutes.

3 Drain the pasta and add to the pan of tomato sauce. Mix well, check the seasoning and serve with the grated Parmesan sprinkled on top.

LAMB STUFFED RED PEPPERS

8½ Points per recipe

Serves 2

Preparation time: 10 minutes

Cooking time: 35–45 minutes

Calories per serving: 285

Freezing: not recommended

Serve with a No Point green vegetable such as broccoli and 100 g (3½ oz) new potatoes for 1 extra Point.

---

2 large red peppers

low fat cooking spray

1 small onion, chopped

1 teaspoon peeled and chopped fresh root ginger

1 garlic clove, crushed

½ teaspoon garam masala

200 g (7 oz) minced lamb

½ green chilli, de-seeded and chopped finely

1 tablespoon chopped fresh coriander

salt and freshly ground black pepper

---

1 Preheat the oven to Gas Mark 4/ 180°C/fan oven 160°C. Halve the peppers, cutting through the stalk. Scoop out the seeds.

2 Spray an ovenproof dish with low fat cooking spray and place the peppers in the dish.

3 Spray a frying pan with low fat cooking spray and fry the onion until golden.

4 Lower the heat and add the ginger, garlic, seasoning and garam masala. Stir fry for 2–3 minutes.

5 Add the minced lamb and fry for about 10–12 minutes. Add the green chilli and chopped fresh coriander and stir fry for another 2–3 minutes.

6 Spoon the lamb mixture into the red peppers. Bake for 15–20 minutes. Serve immediately.

Top tip Always wash your hands and the knife you have been using after chopping chillies, and be careful not to touch your eyes until you have done this – it will burn!

Variation Other coloured peppers or large beefsteak tomatoes could also be used in this recipe – make the filling in the same way and stuff the vegetables before placing in the oven. Tomatoes will take slightly less time to cook. The Points will remain the same.

For a vegetarian version, mix 150 g (5½ oz) cooked couscous with a 5 cm (2 inch) piece of cucumber, finely chopped, 2 tomatoes, finely chopped and 1 tablespoon of chopped fresh coriander. Use to fill the peppers in step 6. The Points will be reduced to 1 per serving.

Lamb Stuffed Red Peppers served with new potatoes: A great mid week supper for 5½ Points per serving.

Great meaty curries and fabulous spicy pizzas, kebabs and stir fries – this chapter has them all, and all for very few Points too! You'll find lots of family favourites with great flavours in this chapter, plus a few new ideas that are just as tasty.

CHICKEN JALFREZI

17 Points per recipe
Serves 4
Preparation time: 10 minutes
Cooking time: 25–30 minutes
Calories per serving: 290
Freezing: recommended for up to 1 month

A real must for all curry lovers, this is quite spicy and absolutely delicious!

low fat cooking spray
1 onion, chopped
2 garlic cloves, crushed
½ teaspoon chilli powder
2 teaspoons curry powder
1 teaspoon tomato purée

4 medium (165 g/5¾ oz) skinless, boneless chicken breasts, cut into chunks
1 teaspoon peeled and grated fresh root ginger
1 green pepper, de-seeded and sliced
125 g (4½ oz) basmati rice
2 shallots, chopped
½ teaspoon turmeric

1 Heat a medium frying pan and spray with low fat cooking spray. Add the onion and garlic and stir fry for 3–4 minutes until starting to soften.

2 Add the spices and tomato purée and cook for another minute, stirring to mix well.

3 Add the chicken breast and ginger and stir to coat the meat with all the spices.

4 Add the pepper, pour in 150 ml (5 fl oz) of water and bring to the boil. Simmer for 15–20 minutes, until the chicken is tender.

5 Cook the rice according to the packet instructions.

6 Meanwhile, spray a frying pan with low fat cooking spray and cook the shallots for 3–4 minutes until starting to soften. Stir in the turmeric and mix well.

7 Add the rice and stir to coat with the turmeric. Continue to stir and cook until all the rice is yellow and hot. Serve with the chicken.

Variation Beef or lamb jalfrezi can be cooked in the same way. Use 600 g (1 lb 5 oz) lean beef steak or lean lamb leg steak. The Points will be 5½ and 5 respectively.

Chicken Jalfrezi:
A hot favourite
for just 4 Points
per serving.

Chicken Chow Mein: Delicious and filling for just 4 Points per serving.

CHICKEN CHOW MEIN

16½ Points per recipe

Serves 4

Preparation time: 10 minutes +
10 minutes marinating

Cooking time: 20 minutes

Calories per serving: 290

Freezing: not recommended

Chow Mein literally means 'stir fried noodles' and can incorporate any meat or vegetable that you wish.

2 medium (165 g/5¾ oz) skinless, boneless chicken breasts, cut into strips

5 teaspoons light soy sauce

1 teaspoon sesame oil

150 g (5½ oz) medium egg noodles

low fat cooking spray

2 garlic cloves, crushed

50 g (1¾ oz) mange tout, shredded

50 g (1¾ oz) wafer thin ham, shredded

salt and freshly ground black pepper

3 spring onions, chopped

2 tablespoons sesame seeds

1 Place the strips of chicken breast in a bowl with 2 teaspoons of the soy sauce and the sesame oil. Leave to marinate for 10 minutes.

2 Add the egg noodles to a pan of boiling, salted water and simmer for 4 minutes; drain and reserve.

3 Spray a wok or large frying pan with low fat cooking spray. Add the chicken strips and stir fry for about 2–3 minutes; then remove.

4 Spray again with low fat cooking spray and quickly stir fry the garlic before adding the mange tout and ham. Stir fry for about 1 minute.

5 Add the noodles, remaining 3 teaspoons of soy sauce, seasoning and spring onions and stir fry for 2 minutes before returning the chicken and any juices to the pan Stir fry for another 3–4 minutes and serve, sprinkled with sesame seeds.

Variation For a vegetarian version replace the chicken with 325 g (11½ oz) Quorn strips – treat in just the same way as the chicken and replace the ham with 50 g (1¾ oz) halved baby sweetcorn. The Points will be 3½ per serving.

CHILLI CON CARNE

18 Points per recipe

Serves 4

Preparation time: 5 minutes

Cooking time: 35–40 minutes

Calories per serving: 290

Freezing: recommended for up to 1 month

Chilli con Carne literally means 'chilli with meat'. This is a delicious low Point version of this great family favourite. Serve with 4 tablespoons of cooked long grain rice for an extra 3 Points per serving.

low fat cooking spray

1 onion, chopped

400 g (14 oz) extra lean minced beef

2 teaspoons chilli powder

1 green pepper, de-seeded and chopped

425 g (15 oz) canned chopped tomatoes

1 tablespoon tomato purée

250 g (9 oz) canned kidney beans, rinsed and drained

salt and freshly ground black pepper

1 Spray a medium pan with low fat cooking spray and sauté the onion for 3–4 minutes, until starting to soften.

2 Add the minced beef and cook for 4–5 minutes, stirring occasionally, to brown the meat.

3 Stir in the chilli powder and green pepper.

4 Pour in the tomatoes, fill the empty can with water and add this to the pan. Stir in the tomato purée, kidney beans and seasoning and bring to the boil. Simmer for 25–30 minutes, stirring occasionally.

Top tip Chilli powder is made from dried red chillies and is used in many spicy dishes. As with chillies in general, add it according to taste.

Variation For a vegetarian alternative, use 300 g (10½ oz) dried split red lentils instead of the meat. Add in step 4 and cook for a further 10–15 minutes until the lentils are tender. The Points will remain the same.

SPICY PORK NOODLES

16 Points per recipe

Serves 4

Preparation time: 10 minutes +
20 minutes chilling

Cooking time: 15 minutes

Calories per serving: 345

Freezing: not recommended

A bowl of spicy noodles with strips of pork and vegetables – a great recipe to serve to friends.

200 g (7 oz) pork tenderloin, cut into strips

225 g (8 oz) egg noodles

low fat cooking spray

3 spring onions

100 g (3½ oz) mange tout

1 red pepper, de-seeded and chopped

75 g (2¾ oz) beansprouts

2 tablespoons chopped fresh coriander

salt

For the marinade

2 tablespoons soy sauce

1 tablespoon honey

1 teaspoon mustard

2 star anise

1 Place the pork in a small bowl and pour in the marinade ingredients. Mix well and chill in the fridge, covered, for at least 20 minutes.

2 Place the egg noodles in a pan of boiling, salted water and cook for 4 minutes. Drain and reserve.

3 Heat a wok or large frying pan and spray with low fat cooking spray. Add the pork and stir fry for 2–3 minutes before adding the spring onions, mange tout and red pepper. Cook for another 3–4 minutes.

4 Add the noodles to the pan and stir well to mix with the pork and vegetables.

5 Finally, add the beansprouts, stir fry for 2–3 minutes and then serve in bowls, sprinkled with chopped coriander.

Top tip Star anise is a flower–shaped pod, brownish black in colour, which adds an aniseed flavour to food.

Variation For a vegetarian alternative replace the pork with 150 g (5½ oz) baby sweetcorn and 2 celery sticks, chopped. Cook these in the same way as the pork. Add 40 g (1½ oz) peanuts at step 5 with the beansprouts. The Points will remain the same.

PORK BIRIYANI

15½ Points per recipe

Serves 4

Preparation time: 12 minutes

Cooking time: 30–35 minutes

Calories per serving: 275

Freezing: not recommended

A Biriyani is an Indian festive dish and is a great one pot meal. Accompany with a crunchy No Point vegetable, such as broccoli or braised celery.

3 tablespoons skimmed milk

2–3 saffron strands

low fat cooking spray

1 large onion, chopped

2 garlic cloves, crushed

1 teaspoon peeled and grated fresh root ginger

1 teaspoon chilli powder

325 g (11½ oz) pork tenderloin, cut into bite size pieces

1 cinnamon stick

2 cardamom pods

2 bay leaves

½ teaspoon cumin seeds

250 g (9 oz) low fat yogurt

300 g (10½ oz) cooked basmati rice

juice of 1 lemon

1 Pour the milk into a jug or bowl and add the saffron strands. Leave to infuse for 10-15 minutes.

2 Meanwhile preheat the oven to Gas Mark 4/180°C/fan oven 160°C.

3 Heat a medium pan and spray with low fat cooking spray. Add the onion and fry until softened then add the garlic, ginger and chilli powder and stir.

4 Add the pork and stir fry for 4–5 minutes, before adding the other spices and herbs.

5 Take off the heat and stir in the yogurt.

6 Layer the rice and the pork mixture in an ovenproof dish – aim for two layers of each. Pour the saffron milk and lemon juice over each layer.

7 Cover and cook for 30–35 minutes until the pork is tender and cooked through.

Variation For a vegetarian alternative use 100 g (3½ oz) broccoli, 100 g (3½ oz) cauliflower, 2 courgettes, 2 carrots and 2 red peppers. Add at step 4. The Points will be 2 per serving.

Spicy Pork Noodles: Spicy, satisfying and only 4 Points per serving.

Saffron Chicken with Apricots: Great fruity flavours for 6 Points per serving!

SAFFRON CHICKEN WITH APRICOTS

6 POINTS

23½ Points per recipe

Serves 4

Preparation time: 10 minutes

Cooking time: 25–30 minutes

Calories per serving: 415

Freezing: recommended for up to
1 month

a pinch of saffron threads

250 ml (9 fl oz) hot chicken stock

low fat cooking spray

1 large onion, sliced

2 garlic cloves, sliced

2 medium (165 g/5¾ oz) skinless,
boneless chicken breasts, chopped
into bite size pieces

1 teaspoon ground cumin

1 teaspoon turmeric

1 teaspoon ground coriander

1 teaspoon paprika

75 g (2¾ oz) dried apricots, halved

150 g (5½ oz) canned chick peas

175 g (6 oz) couscous

1 tablespoon chopped fresh mint

1 tablespoon chopped fresh parsley

salt and freshly ground black pepper

50 g (1¾ oz) flaked almonds, toasted,
to serve

1 Stir the saffron threads into the chicken stock and leave to one side.

2 Heat a medium pan, spray with low fat cooking spray and sauté the onion and garlic for 3–4 minutes until starting to soften.

3 Add the chicken pieces and cook for another 3–4 minutes, stirring occasionally. Add all the spices and stir to coat the chicken.

4 Pour in the stock and saffron and add the apricots and chick peas. Bring to a simmer and continue to simmer for 15–20 minutes, until the chicken is cooked through.

5 Meanwhile, place the couscous in a large bowl and add just enough boiling water to cover. Leave to stand for 10 minutes. Just before serving, stir briskly with a fork to break up any lumps.

6 Check the seasoning of the chicken and stir in the chopped herbs. Serve on a bed of couscous sprinkled with the toasted almond flakes.

THAI BEEF SALAD

2 POINTS

17 Points per recipe
Serves 8
Preparation time: 15 minutes
Cooking time: 5 minutes
Calories per serving: 135
Freezing: not recommended

A warm salad with a touch of spice! This is a great lunch party dish.

low fat cooking spray
500 g (1 lb 2 oz) lean beef fillet steak, cut into strips
2 garlic cloves, chopped finely
2 cm (³/₄ inch) piece of fresh root ginger, peeled and chopped finely
1 green chilli, de-seeded and chopped finely
juice of 1 lemon
1 tablespoon fish sauce (nam pla)
2 × 300g (10¹/₂ oz) ripe mangoes, peeled and chopped
¹/₂ large cucumber, cut into strips
100 g (3¹/₂ oz) beansprouts
1 iceburg lettuce, shredded

1 Heat a wok or large frying pan and spray with low fat cooking spray. Add the steak, garlic, ginger and chilli and stir fry over a high heat for 3–4 minutes.

2 Pour in the lemon juice and fish sauce and continue to stir fry until the juices are sizzling.

3 Remove from the heat and lift out the steak with a slotted spoon. Place in a bowl with the remaining ingredients and toss together.

4 Place on a large platter and pour over the liquid from the wok.

Variation Try replacing the beef with the same quantity of prawns. The Points will be 1¹/₂ per serving.

SPICY PIZZA

6¹/₂ POINTS

26 Points per recipe
Serves 4
Preparation time: 10 minutes + 1–1¹/₂ hours standing time + 15 minutes
Cooking time: 8–10 minutes
Calories per serving: 390
Freezing: not recommended

A great recipe for all your friends to enjoy!

200 g (7 oz) strong white bread flour
¹/₂ teaspoon salt
125 ml (4 fl oz) tepid water
¹/₂ teaspoon dried yeast
low fat cooking spray

For the topping
1 onion, chopped
400 g (14 oz) canned, chopped tomatoes
1 teaspoon dried oregano
100 g (3¹/₂ oz) chorizo slices
1 red pepper, sliced thinly
50 g (1³/₄ oz) mozzarella light, sliced
100 g (3¹/₂ oz) half fat Cheddar, grated
salt and freshly ground black pepper
No Point salad, to serve

1 Place the flour and salt in a large bowl. Make a well in the centre and add the tepid water.

2 Sprinkle over the yeast and leave to stand for 5 minutes.

3 Stir to dissolve the yeast and gradually draw in the flour to make a soft dough.

4 Turn out on to a floured surface and knead the dough until smooth.

5 Place the dough in a clean bowl that has been sprayed with low fat cooking spray, cover and leave to rise until doubled in size, about 1–1¹/₂ hours.

6 Meanwhile, to make the tomato sauce for the topping, heat a frying pan and spray with low fat cooking spray. Cook the onion for 3–4 minutes until starting to soften, then add the tomatoes and oregano. Season well and cook for 8–10 minutes until slightly thickened.

7 Punch the dough to take out the air.

8 Shape the dough into a ball, cover with a cloth and leave to rest for 10 minutes.

9 Place the dough on to a lightly floured surface and roll into a 30 cm (12 inch) round. Place on a baking sheet.

10 Preheat the oven to its hottest temperature and place a shelf near the top.

11 Spread the pizza with the tomato sauce and then lay the slices of chorizo and the red pepper on top.

12 Finally, top with the slices of mozzarella and grated half fat Cheddar. Bake in the oven for 8–10 minutes until the base is golden and the cheese is bubbling. Serve immediately, with a No Point salad.

Variation If you prefer your pizzas really hot, sprinkle over a few slices of green chilli.

STIR FRIED BEEF WITH BLACK BEAN SAUCE

8½ Points per recipe

Serves 4
Preparation time: 10 minutes
Cooking time: 15–20 minutes
Calories per serving: 155
Freezing: not recommended

Stir frying is so quick, and with lots of great sauces available it's the perfect way to make a delicious low Point meal. Serve with steamed pak choi.

low fat cooking spray
300 g (10½ oz) lean beef fillet steak, cut into small bite size pieces
1 onion, sliced
2 garlic cloves, crushed
2 cm (¾ inch) piece of fresh root ginger, peeled and chopped
1 yellow pepper, de-seeded and sliced
150 g (5½ oz) green beans, cut in half
4 tablespoons black bean sauce

1 Heat a wok or large frying pan and spray with low fat cooking spray. Add the pieces of beef and stir fry for 5–6 minutes, until browned. Remove with a slotted spoon.
2 To the wok, add the onion, garlic and ginger and stir fry for 4–5 minutes before adding the pepper and green beans. Stir fry for another 2–3 minutes.
3 Return the beef to the wok with the black bean sauce and 100 ml (3½ fl oz) of water.
4 Stir fry for another 5–6 minutes, until the beef is cooked and the sauce has thickened.

Top tip For stir frying, always make sure your wok or frying pan is quite hot before adding the first ingredient.

Variation For a No Point vegetarian version, omit the beef and replace with 300 g (10½ oz), of No Point vegetables of your choice, e.g. courgette, broccoli and red pepper all sliced thinly.

LEMON CHICKEN

14½ Points per recipe

Serves 4
Preparation time: 12 minutes + 20 minutes chilling time
Cooking time: 20 minutes
Calories per serving: 265
Freezing: recommended for up to 1 month

A delicate chicken recipe, with a little spice and a hint of lemon.

2 medium (165 g/5¾ oz) skinless, boneless chicken breasts, cut into thin strips
1 egg white, beaten
½ teaspoon salt
2½ teaspoons cornflour
65 ml (2½ fl oz) chicken stock
3 tablespoons freshly squeezed lemon juice
1 teaspoon artificial sweetener
1 tablespoon soy sauce
2 garlic cloves, crushed
½ teaspoon chilli flakes
low fat cooking spray
2 leeks, sliced
150 g (5½ oz) basmati rice
1 teaspoon sesame oil
2 spring onions, chopped

1 Mix together the chicken strips, egg white, salt and 1½ teaspoons of cornflour in a bowl and then leave to chill in the fridge for 20 minutes.
2 Bring a medium pan of water to the boil and drop in the chicken strips. Cook for 1–2 minutes until the chicken turns completely white. Drain it and leave to one side.
3 In a wok or large frying pan, mix together the chicken stock, lemon juice, sweetener, soy sauce, garlic and chilli flakes. Blend the remaining teaspoon of cornflour with a teaspoon of water to a paste and mix the paste into the sauce. Bring to the boil and, when the mixture starts to thicken, add the chicken and cook for 6–8 minutes, stirring occasionally.
4 Meanwhile, spray another saucepan with low fat cooking spray and fry the sliced leeks for 3–4 minutes. Stir in the rice and pour in enough water to cover. Bring to the boil and simmer for 8–10 minutes, until the rice is cooked.
5 Pour the sesame oil into the chicken mixture and sprinkle with spring onions.
6 Drain the rice and leeks and divide between four plates. Spoon over the chicken and serve immediately.

Stir fried Beef with Black Bean Sauce: A Friday night favourite for just 2 Points per serving.

**Lamb Koftas:
A delicious
barbecue recipe
for only 3
Points per
skewer.**

LAMB KOFTAS

3 POINTS

29½ Points per recipe

Makes 10

Preparation time: 15 minutes +
20 minutes chilling

Cooking time: 12–15 minutes

Calories per skewer: 155

Freezing: not recommended

A great recipe for a summer lunch –
skewers of spicy lamb that can be
cooked on the barbecue and served
with a crunchy No Point salad.

For the koftas

500 g (1 lb 2 oz) minced lamb

1 egg yolk

100 g (3½ oz) fresh white breadcrumbs

1 onion, chopped

1 tablespoon chopped fresh parsley

½ teaspoon ground cinnamon

1 teaspoon ground cumin

½ teaspoon chilli powder

1 teaspoon turmeric

½ teaspoon ground allspice

For the sauce

150 g (5½ oz) low fat plain yogurt

juice of ½ lemon

1 tablespoon tahini paste

2 garlic cloves, crushed

1 Soak 10 wooden kebab skewers
in water for at least 30 minutes.

2 Place all the kofta ingredients in
a food processor and blend until
completely mixed.

3 Using your hands, form the mixture
into balls and squeeze on to the end
of the skewers. Place on a plate or
tray and cover with cling film. Leave
to chill in the fridge for 20 minutes.

4 In a bowl, mix together the sauce
ingredients and place in the fridge
until ready to serve.

5 Heat the grill until quite hot and
cook the koftas for about 12–15
minutes, turning quite often to
prevent them from burning. If using
a barbecue the same applies – keep
checking them to prevent burning.

6 Serve with the tahini and yogurt
sauce.

Top tip Soaking the kebab skewers
prevents them from burning when
the koftas are cooking.

CHICKEN KORMA

6½ POINTS

26 Points per recipe

Serves 4

Preparation time: 12 minutes

Cooking time: 15–20 minutes

Calories per serving: 420

Freezing: recommended for up to
1 month

A favourite for those who like their
curries creamy and not too hot!

low fat cooking spray

1 onion, chopped

2 garlic cloves, crushed

½ teaspoon chilli powder

½ teaspoon turmeric

½ teaspoon ground coriander

1 teaspoon ground cumin

1 green cardamom pod, crushed

a pinch of salt

500 g (1 lb 2 oz) skinless, boneless
chicken breasts, cut into bitesize pieces

1 teaspoon tomato purée

1 teaspoon peeled and grated fresh
root ginger

½ teaspoon garam masala

400 ml (14 fl oz) chicken stock

250 g (9 oz) basmati rice

100 ml (3½ fl oz) reduced fat
coconut milk

25 g (1 oz) flaked almonds

salt and freshly ground black pepper

1 Heat a medium pan and spray
with low fat cooking spray. Add
the onion and garlic and cook for
2–3 minutes.

2 Add the spices, salt and chicken
and stir well to completely coat the
chicken.

3 Add the tomato puree, ginger,
garam masala and chicken stock and
bring to the boil. Simmer gently for
15 minutes. Cook the rice according
to the packet instructions.

4 Add the coconut milk and flaked
almonds and continue to simmer
for another 5 minutes. Check the
seasoning and serve with the cooked
basmati rice.

Variation For Prawn Korma, omit the
chicken and use 400 g (14 oz) of
prawns instead. The Points per
serving will be 6.

vegetarian
dishes

Probably the most colourful of foods we eat, vegetables are full of essential vitamins and minerals, and many have no Points at all. You'll find lots of inspiring ways to spice up your veggies, so indulge yourself with some satisfying, fantastic flavours, knowing that you are enjoying a healthy, energy giving meal.

JUNGLE CURRY

10½ Points per recipe

 Serves 6

Preparation time: 15 minutes
Cooking time: 15–18 minutes
Calories per serving: 185
Freezing: recommended for up to one month

A great curry with lots of crunchy vegetables – the perfect spicy vegetarian dish!

200 g (7 oz) long grain rice

low fat cooking spray

2 garlic cloves, crushed

2 cm (³/₄ inch) piece of fresh root ginger, peeled and chopped

1 lemon grass stick, chopped finely

1 teaspoon chilli flakes

1 teaspoon curry paste

1 large red onion, chopped

125 g (4½ oz) sugar snap peas

2 red peppers, de-seeded and chopped

100 g (3½ oz) baby corn, cut in half

2 medium courgettes, sliced

125 g (4½ oz) chestnut mushrooms

125 g (4½ oz) green beans

100 ml (3½ fl oz) vegetable stock

1 tablespoon soy sauce

150 g (5½ oz) fresh spinach

1 Cook the rice according to the packet instructions.
2 Heat a wok or large frying pan and spray with low fat cooking spray. Stir fry the garlic, ginger and lemon grass for 2–3 minutes before stirring in the chilli flakes and curry paste.
3 Add the red onion, sugar snap peas, red peppers and baby corn and cook for 3–4 minutes, stirring constantly.

4 Add the courgettes, chestnut mushrooms and green beans and then pour in the stock and soy sauce. Bring to the boil and continue to stir fry for a further 4–5 minutes.
5 Finally, add the spinach and stir fry for a further 4–5 minutes until the spinach has wilted and the other vegetables are softening.
6 Serve the curry in warmed bowls with the cooked rice.

Top tip Always cut away the outer leaves of lemon grass and only use the inner ones – the outer leaves are very tough.

Jungle Curry:
Fabulous Eastern
flavours – for just
2 Points per
serving.

VEGETABLE COCONUT STIR FRY

4½ POINTS

18½ Points per recipe

Ⓥ Ⓥ̲ *Serves 4*

Preparation time: 5 minutes

Cooking time: 15–20 minutes

Calories per serving: 285

Freezing: not recommended

A tasty, colourful and quick vegetarian dish – perfect for entertaining at the last minute!

110 g (4 oz) basmati rice

low fat cooking spray

2 cm (³/4 inch) piece of fresh root ginger, peeled and grated

2 garlic cloves, crushed

½ teaspoon ground coriander

500 g (1 lb 2 oz) No Point stir fry vegetables, e.g. courgette, carrot, broccoli, beansprouts, leeks and mange tout

125 g (4½ oz) fresh baby spinach or pak choi

50 g (1³/4 oz) shredded or desiccated coconut

a bunch of fresh coriander, chopped

salt and freshly ground black pepper

2 tablespoons sesame seeds, to garnish

1 Cook the rice according to the packet instructions.

2 Heat the low fat cooking spray in a wok or large frying pan. Stir in the fresh ginger, garlic and ground coriander and cook for 1–2 minutes.

3 Add the stir fry vegetables and stir fry for 12–15 minutes.

4 Stir in the spinach or pak choi and cook until it has wilted. Check the seasoning.

5 Sprinkle with the coconut and chopped coriander and serve immediately on a bed of cooked basmati rice, sprinkled with sesame seeds.

Variation For those that love seafood, 125 g (4½ oz) prawns could be added to this dish at the same time as the spinach. The Points per serving will then be 5.

Spicy Bean Hotpot: A quick and satisfying hot lunch for just 2½ Points per serving.

SPICY BEAN HOTPOT

2½ POINTS

10½ Points per recipe

Ⓥ Ⓥ̲ *Serves 4*

Preparation time: 15 minutes

Cooking time: 20–30 minutes

Calories per serving: 175

Freezing: recommended

low fat cooking spray

1 red onion, chopped

2 carrots, peeled and chopped

2 celery sticks, chopped

1 red pepper, de-seeded and chopped

1 teaspoon ground cumin

1 teaspoon curry powder

½ teaspoon ground ginger

415 g (14½ oz) canned Weight Watchers from Heinz Baked Beans

420 g (14³/4 oz) canned red kidney beans, rinsed and drained

salt and freshly ground black pepper

a bunch of fresh parsley, chopped, to garnish

1 Heat a medium saucepan and spray with low fat cooking spray. Add the onion, carrots, celery and red pepper and cook for 4–5 minutes, stirring occasionally.

2 Add the spices and mix well. Cook for another 1–2 minutes.

3 Pour in the baked beans and kidney beans and 200 ml (7 fl oz) of water. Bring to the boil and then simmer, covered, for 15 minutes.

4 Check the seasoning and sprinkle in the parsley before serving in big bowls.

Variation For those that miss their meat, you can add bacon or low fat sausages to this dish. Chop 100 g (3½ oz) bacon or low fat sausages and add with the vegetables at the beginning. The Points per serving if using bacon will be 4 and if using sausages 3½.

SPICY TOFU COURGETTES

1 POINT

2 Points per recipe

Ⓥ Ⓥⓔ *Serves 2*

Preparation time: 5 minutes
Cooking time: 12 minutes
Calories per serving: 95
Freezing: not recommended

A quick and tasty vegetarian dish for two.

low fat cooking spray
2 garlic cloves, crushed
2 cm (³/₄ inch) piece of fresh root ginger, peeled and finely chopped
1 star anise
2 medium courgettes, sliced thickly
2 spring onions, sliced
1 teaspoon cornflour
125 ml (4 fl oz) vegetable stock
125 g (4¹/₂ oz) tofu, cut into cubes
salt and freshly ground black pepper

1 Heat the low fat cooking spray in a frying pan or wok and stir fry the garlic and ginger for 1–2 minutes.
2 Add the star anise, courgette and spring onions and fry for 1 minute.
3 Place the cornflour in a small bowl or cup and stir in 1 tablespoon of the stock to make a smooth paste – leave to one side.
4 Pour the remaining stock into the wok or frying pan, season and bring to a simmer. Cook for 4–5 minutes.
5 Remove the courgette with a slotted spoon, and then add the tofu to the pan. Cook for 2–3 minutes before pouring in the cornflour mixture. Stir well until the mixture thickens then return the courgettes to the pan.
6 Check the seasoning and serve.

Top tip Tofu is the Japanese name for bean curd – a pale soft cheese like substance that is made from soya bean milk.

Variation Other No Point vegetables can be cooked in this way – try broccoli or carrots. The Points will remain the same.

Spicy Tofu Courgettes: Fast and filling for only 1 Point per serving!

WARM CHICK PEA, CHILLI AND FETA SALAD

5¹/₂ POINTS

23 Points per recipe

Ⓥ *Serves 4*

Preparation time: 20 minutes + 20 minutes standing
Calories per serving: 230
Freezing: not recommended

A great tasting and satisfying salad which combines hot chillies and garlic with creamy feta cheese and chick peas.

1 teaspoon olive oil
1 red chilli, de-seeded and sliced finely
4 garlic cloves, crushed
2 red onions, sliced finely
2 tablespoons cider vinegar
2 × 450 g cans of chick peas, drained and rinsed
a handful of roughly chopped fresh coriander
a handful of roughly chopped fresh flat leaf parsley
75 g (2³/₄ oz) feta cheese, crumbled
3 spring onions, sliced
a handful of roughly chopped fresh mint

To serve
iceberg lettuce, shredded
watercress

1 Heat the olive oil in a frying pan and stir fry the chilli, garlic and red onions for about 5–6 minutes. Add the vinegar and boil until it has nearly evaporated.
2 Put the chick peas and the onion mixture into a large bowl and, while still warm, add the remaining ingredients.
3 Mix well and leave to stand for 20 minutes before serving – this will allow the flavours to develop.
4 Serve on a bed of iceberg lettuce and watercress.

Red and Green
Pepper Burritos:
A delicious
Mexican meal for
just 4 Points per
serving.

RED AND GREEN
PEPPER BURRITOS

(4 POINTS)

15 Points per recipe

 Serves 4

Preparation time: 15 minutes

Cooking time: 15–17 minutes

Calories per serving: 255

Freezing: not recommended

A delicious vegetarian version of this
popular Mexican dish. Serve with a
crunchy No Point green salad.

low fat cooking spray

1 large onion, sliced

1/2 teaspoon chilli powder

1 red pepper, de-seeded and sliced

1 green pepper, de-seeded and sliced

*100 g (3¹/2 oz) canned red kidney
beans, drained*

4 soft flour tortillas

100 g (3¹/2 oz) low fat plain yogurt

*75 g (2³/4 oz) half fat Cheddar cheese,
grated*

1 Heat the low fat cooking spray in
a large frying pan. Add the onion
and sauté for 2–3 minutes on a
gentle heat.

2 Add the chilli powder and stir well
before adding the red and green
peppers. Cook for another 8–10
minutes, stirring occasionally until
the peppers have softened and the
onion is starting to caramelise slightly.

3 Add the kidney beans and cook
for 3–4 minutes.

4 Preheat the grill.

5 Heat the flour tortillas according
to the pack instructions.

6 Divide the low fat yogurt between
the 4 tortillas, spreading it over the
centre of each one. Divide the
pepper mixture between the tortillas
and wrap or fold each one and place
in a shallow heatproof dish.

7 Sprinkle the burritos with the
grated cheese and place under the
grill until the cheese is bubbling
and melted.

VEGETABLE THAI CURRY

16½ Points per recipe

Ⓥ Ⓥⓖ Serves 4

Preparation time: 12 minutes

Cooking time: 30–35 minutes

Calories per serving: 270

Freezing: recommended for up to
1 month.

A delicious vegetable curry that
captures the delicate flavours of
Thai cooking.

1 small butternut squash, peeled and
cut into bite size pieces

2 carrots, peeled and cut into bite
size pieces

2 courgettes, cut into bite size pieces

165 g (5¾ oz) broccoli, broken into
florets

1 red onion, chopped into bite size
pieces

1 teaspoon cumin seeds

low fat cooking spray

110 g (4 oz) Thai fragrant rice

1 lemon grass stick, outer leaves
removed , inside chopped finely

2 garlic cloves, crushed

2 cm (¾ inch) piece of fresh root
ginger, peeled and chopped

1 teaspoon vegetarian red Thai
curry paste

3 tablespoons crunchy peanut butter,
blended with 100 ml (3½ fl oz)
boiling water

1 Preheat the oven to Gas Mark 6/
200°C/fan oven 180°C.

2 Mix together all the chopped
vegetables and the cumin seeds in
a roasting tin. Spray with low fat
cooking spray and roast in the oven
for 25 minutes.

3 Cook the rice according to the
packet instructions.

4 After 25 minutes, heat a wok or
large frying pan with low fat cooking
spray and stir fry the lemon grass,
garlic and ginger for 3–4 minutes.

5 Stir in the red Thai curry paste and
then add the roasted vegetables.

6 Pour over the blended peanut
butter and bring to a simmer. Cook
for 2–3 minutes then serve with
Thai fragrant rice.

Top tip Roasting the vegetables first
makes their flavours more intense
and gives slightly more bite. It also
gives you time to do something else!

ONION AND ROSEMARY TARTE TATIN

32½ Points per recipe

Ⓥ Serves 6

Preparation time: 20–25 minutes

Cooking time: 15 minutes

Calories per serving: 250

Freezing: not recommended

A really tasty tart – caramelised onions
with a hint of rosemary, on top of
luscious, light puff pastry. Serve with
a crisp, No Point green salad.

low fat cooking spray

1 large onion, halved and sliced thickly

1 large red onion, halved and sliced
thickly

2 garlic cloves, sliced

leaves from 3–4 fresh rosemary sprigs

350 g (12 oz) ready made puff pastry

salt and freshly ground black pepper

1 Preheat the oven to Gas Mark 7/
220°C/Fan oven 200°C.

2 Heat the low fat cooking spray in
a medium pan and add the onions
and garlic. When they start to cook

turn the heat down to very low and
cover the pan. Cook for 15–20
minutes, stirring occasionally, until
they start to caramelise. Season well.

3 Add the rosemary to the pan and
stir in. Pour the onion mixture into
a 23 cm (9 inch) flan tin.

4 Roll out the pastry and cut to fit
the tin. Place on top of the onions
and tuck in the edges.

5 Bake for 12–15 minutes until the
top is golden.

6 Turn out on to a plate so the
onions are on top. Serve warm.

Aubergine Madras:
Ideal for those who
like it spicy – 4½
Points per serving.

AUBERGINE MADRAS

18 Points per recipe

(V) (VG) Serves 4

Preparation time: 15 minutes
Cooking time: 25–30 minutes
Calories per serving: 290
Freezing: not recommended

Madras has come to be known as a very hot curry in this country – this recipe is no exception!

1 teaspoon coriander seeds
½ teaspoon fennel seeds
½ teaspoon peppercorns
2 cloves
1 teaspoon chilli flakes
low fat cooking spray

1 large onion, sliced
1 garlic clove, crushed
1 teaspoon peeled and grated fresh root ginger
2 aubergines, cut into chunks
2 tomatoes, chopped
200 ml (7 fl oz) reduced fat coconut milk
salt and freshly ground black pepper
250 g (9 oz) basmati rice

1 Heat a non stick frying pan over a medium heat and add the coriander and fennel seeds, peppercorns, cloves and chilli flakes. Heat until they start to darken and you can smell the aroma. Leave to cool and then grind in a coffee grinder or with a pestle and mortar.

2 Heat the low fat cooking spray in a medium pan and cook the onion and garlic, for 4–5 minutes until starting to soften.

3 Add the ginger, aubergines and tomatoes and stir well before adding the spice mixture. Stir well again then pour in the coconut milk. Bring to the boil, cover and simmer for 10 minutes. Meanwhile cook the rice according to the packet instructions.

4 Uncover and cook for another 10–15 minutes, until the aubergine is tender and the juices have started to thicken slightly. Check the seasoning and serve with the cooked basmati rice.

SWEET POTATO AND PEA TAGINE

15½ Points per recipe

(V) (VG) Serves 4

Preparation time: 10 minutes
Cooking time: 30 minutes
Calories per serving: 285
Freezing: recommended for up to 1 month

A delicious North African dish that is normally cooked in a traditional shallow earthenware cooking pot called a tagine.

2 tablespoons lemon juice
2 teaspoons honey
1 teaspoon ground cinnamon
½ teaspoon chilli powder
low fat cooking spray
1 large onion, sliced
2 garlic cloves, sliced

750 g (1 lb 10 oz) sweet potato, cut into bite size pieces
100 g (3½ oz) frozen or canned peas
salt
2 medium pitta breads, to serve

1 In a small bowl or jug, mix together 1 tablespoon of the lemon juice with the honey, cinnamon and chilli powder. Leave to one side.

2 Heat a medium pan and spray with low fat cooking spray. Add the onion and garlic and cook for 4–5 minutes, until starting to soften.

3 Add the sweet potato and the honey and lemon juice mixture and stir really well.

4 Pour in the remaining lemon juice and 200 ml (7 fl oz) of water and season with salt. Bring to the boil and then simmer for 15 minutes.

5 Add the peas and bring back to a simmer for another 10 minutes, or until the sweet potato is tender.

6 Serve with toasted pitta bread cut into slices, for dipping in the sauce.

Variation Substitute butternut squash for the sweet potato. The Points per serving will then be 1½.

Sweet Potato and Pea Tagine: Traditional Moroccan flavours for only 4 Points per serving.

fish
dishes

You'll find lots of fabulous fish recipes in this chapter that are all delicious, low in Points and so easy to prepare. From great summer barbecue recipes to warming winter stews, there's something here to spice up your cooking all through the year!

CHILLI SEAFOOD SPAGHETTI

4 POINTS

16½ Points per recipe

Serves 4

Preparation time: 6 minutes

Cooking time: 10 minutes

Calories per serving: 305

Freezing: not recommended

A great pasta dish with a lovely spicy tomato and seafood sauce.

200 g (7 oz) spaghetti

low fat cooking spray

1 onion, chopped

¼ teaspoon chilli flakes

400 g (14 oz) canned chopped tomatoes

300 g (10½ oz) mixed seafood

2 tablespoons chopped fresh parsley

salt and freshly ground black pepper

50 g (1¾ oz) half fat Cheddar cheese, grated, to serve

1 Bring a pan of salted water to the boil and then add the spaghetti and cook for 6–8 minutes until al dente (tender but still with a slight 'bite').

2 Meanwhile in another pan, heat the low fat cooking spray and sauté the onion for 3–4 minutes and then add the chilli flakes.

3 Pour in the chopped tomatoes and cook for 1–2 minutes. Then add the mixed seafood. Stir in the chopped parsley.

4 When the pasta is cooked, drain and add to the seafood mixture. Toss gently to coat the pasta with the sauce, check the seasoning, and then divide between four pasta bowls. Sprinkle with the grated cheese and serve immediately.

Top tip If you like your food slightly hotter, just add more chilli flakes.

Variation This can be made into a more substantial meal by adding 50 g (1¾ oz) of prawns or chopped salami. The Points per serving will be 4½ if using prawns or 5½ if using salami.

Chilli Seafood Spaghetti: Quick, tasty and only 4 Points per serving.

Spicy Crab Cakes: Enjoy the flavours of the Orient for just 1 Point per serving.

SPICY CRAB CAKES

1 POINT

4½ Points per recipe

Serves 4

Preparation time: 30 minutes +
20 minutes chilling

Cooking time: 12–16 minutes

Calories per serving: 90

Freezing: not recommended

These tasty crab cakes are perfect for a light lunch or served as a starter for a dinner party for friends. Serve with a green No Point salad.

150 g (5½ oz) potatoes, peeled
250 g (9 oz) crabmeat
3 spring onions, sliced
½ teaspoon cayenne pepper
1 teaspoon wholegrain mustard
½ red pepper, de-seeded and chopped finely
grated zest and juice of ½ lime
1 tablespoon chopped fresh coriander
low fat cooking spray
salt and freshly ground black pepper

1 Bring a small pan of salted water to the boil and add the potatoes. Cook for 8–10 minutes until tender. Drain and leave to cool.

2 Place the remaining ingredients, except the low fat cooking spray, in a bowl.

3 When the potatoes are cool enough to handle, grate them into the bowl.

4 Mix well and shape into 8 cakes. Place on a plate or tray and chill for 20 minutes.

5 Heat a frying pan sprayed with low fat cooking spray and add the crab cakes. Cook for 3–4 minutes on each side.

TROUT STUFFED WITH COUSCOUS, ALMONDS AND HERBS

7 POINTS

28½ Points per recipe

Serves 4

Preparation time: 25 minutes

Cooking time: 15–20 minutes

Calories per serving: 450

Freezing: not recommended

A very impressive Moroccan inspired dish, where the couscous and spices are cooked inside the fish. Serve with a fresh, light No Point salad.

low fat cooking spray
1 small onion, chopped finely
2 garlic cloves, crushed
1 teaspoon ground cumin
100 g (3½ oz) couscous
300 ml (½ pint) vegetable stock
1 tablespoon chopped fresh parsley
2 tablespoons chopped fresh mint
4 trout, 200 g (7 oz) each, gutted, heads removed and boned
40 g (1½ oz) flaked almonds, chopped
salt and freshly ground black pepper

1 Preheat the oven to Gas Mark 6/ 200°C/fan oven 180°C.

2 Heat a frying pan and spray with low fat cooking spray. Fry the onion for 2–3 minutes, until softened.

3 Add the garlic and cumin and cook for 1 minute more.

4 Add the couscous, vegetable stock and herbs and stir well. Bring to the boil then remove from the heat and leave for 10–15 minutes, to allow the couscous to absorb the stock.

5 Season the trout and fill each one with the couscous.

6 Place the fish in a shallow baking dish that has been sprayed with low fat cooking spray. Sprinkle with the chopped almonds.

7 Bake in the oven for 15–20 minutes until the fish is tender.

PAN FRIED SALMON WITH GINGER AND GARLIC

4 POINTS

8½ Points per recipe

Serves 2

Preparation time: 15 minutes

Cooking time: 25 minutes

Calories per serving: 305

Freezing: not recommended

A quick and tasty way to serve salmon.

2 × 100 g (3½ oz) salmon fillets
low fat cooking spray
2 garlic cloves
1 cm (½ inch) piece of fresh root ginger, peeled and grated
3 spring onions, chopped
2 tablespoons soy sauce
2 teaspoons lemon juice
125 g (4½ oz) bok choy
salt and freshly ground black pepper
2 tablespoons sesame seeds, to garnish

1 Dry the salmon fillets with kitchen roll. Sprinkle the skin side with salt and pepper.

2 Spray a frying pan with low fat cooking spray and heat until hot.

3 Place the salmon fillets in the frying pan skin side down and cook for 6–8 minutes, until the skin is slightly charred. Turn the fillets over and immediately add the garlic, ginger and spring onions.

4 Pour over the soy sauce, this will start to sizzle, and then add the lemon juice and remove the pan from the heat. The heat from the frying pan will continue to cook the salmon for the next couple of minutes.

5 Steam the bok choy for 8 minutes and serve the salmon on a bed of this, sprinkled with sesame seeds.

Variation Try chunky tuna steaks or even flaky cod fillets. The Points per serving for both will be 2½.

SEAFOOD GOAN CURRY

15 Points per recipe

Serves 4
Preparation time: 10 minutes
Cooking time: 20 minutes
Calories per serving: 245
Freezing: not recommended

Goa is an area on the west coast of Indian where fish and seafood is what the locals thrive on. This recipe uses some of the wonderful spices available there.

110 g (4 oz) basmati rice
1 teaspoon paprika
1 teaspoon cayenne pepper
¼ teaspoon turmeric
1 tablespoon ground coriander
1 teaspoon ground cumin
1 tablespoon lemon juice
½ teaspoon salt
low fat cooking spray
½ teaspoon mustard seeds
1 onion, chopped
2 garlic cloves, sliced
200 ml (7 fl oz) reduced fat coconut milk
350 g (12 oz) mixed seafood
bunch of fresh coriander, chopped

1 Cook the basmati rice according to the packet instructions.

2 In a small bowl mix together the paprika, cayenne pepper, turmeric, coriander, cumin and lemon juice. Then add the salt and 1 tablespoon of water to the bowl and leave to one side.

3 Heat a frying pan and spray with low fat cooking spray. Add the mustard seeds and when they start popping add the onion and garlic. Cook for 4–5 minutes until they start to turn golden.

4 Pour in the spice mixture and cook for 1–2 minutes, stirring.

5 Pour the coconut milk into the pan and simmer for 4–5 minutes. Add the seafood to the pan and simmer for another 3–4 minutes. Serve sprinkled with chopped fresh coriander, with the basmati rice.

Variation For a prawn curry use this recipe in exactly the same way, substituting the same weight of prawns for the seafood. The Points per serving will remain the same.

MARINATED SARDINES WITH TOMATO RELISH

32½ Points per recipe

Serves 6
Preparation time: 20 minutes + marinating
Cooking time: 5 minutes
Calories per serving: 210
Freezing: not recommended

A delicious way to serve fish all through the year, but especially in the summer when they can be popped on the barbecue!

12 sardines, gutted, about 90 g (3¼ oz) each

For the marinade
1½ tablespoons chopped fresh coriander
1½ tablespoons chopped fresh parsley
3 garlic cloves, crushed
1 teaspoon ground cumin
1 teaspoon ground coriander
2 teaspoons paprika
a pinch of saffron threads
a pinch of dried chilli flakes
grated rind and juice of 1 lemon

For the relish
4 spring onions
juice of 1 lime
250 g (9 oz) tomatoes, skinned, de-seeded and chopped
½ dried red chilli, de-seeded and chopped
3 tablespoons chopped fresh coriander

1 To make the marinade, mix all the ingredients together in a bowl.

2 Put the sardines in a glass dish and pour over the marinade. Turn the fish so they are completely coated in the marinade and then leave in the fridge for at least 1 hour.

3 To make the relish, place all the relish ingredients in a food processor or blender and blend briefly to give a chunky relish.

4 Heat the grill (or barbecue) and cook the sardines for 3–4 minutes on each side. Serve immediately with the tomato relish.

Top tips Sardines smaller than about 13 cm (5 inches) long do not need to be gutted.

You can make the relish earlier and store in the fridge, but leave to stand out of the fridge while you cook the sardines.

SWEET AND SOUR PRAWNS

2 POINTS

8½ Points per recipe

Serves 4
Preparation time: 20 minutes
Cooking time: 10 minutes
Calories per serving: 220
Freezing: not recommended

A delicious, low Point version of this popular Chinese dish.

110 g (4 oz) basmati rice
low fat cooking spray
2 garlic cloves, sliced

2 cm (¾ inch) piece of fresh root ginger, peeled and chopped
5 spring onions, chopped into long pieces
1 red pepper, de-seeded and cut into square pieces
250 g (9 oz) raw, peeled tiger prawns
200 g (7 oz) canned water chestnuts

For the sauce

100 ml (3½ fl oz) fish stock
3 tablespoons soy sauce
1 tablespoon rice vinegar
1 tablespoon tomato purée
2 teaspoons artificial sweetener
1 teaspoon cornflour, mixed with
3 teaspoons water

1 Cook the basmati rice according to the packet instructions.

2 Heat the low fat cooking spray in a wok or large frying pan. Add the garlic, ginger, spring onions and red pepper and stir fry for 4–5 minutes.

3 Add the prawns and water chestnuts and cook for 1 minute.

4 Mix together all the sauce ingredients and pour into the wok. Stir fry for 3–4 minutes until the sauce starts to thicken.

5 Serve with the basmati rice.

Top tip Water chestnuts are a white, sweet, crunchy bulb about the size of a walnut and are sold in many supermarkets and Chinese grocers.

Sweet and Sour Prawns: A takeaway favourite for just 2½ Points.

Fish with a Spicy Crust: A delicious combination for just 2½ Points!

FISH WITH A SPICY CRUST

2½ POINTS

5½ Points per recipe

Serves 2

Preparation time: 8 minutes

Cooking time: 20-25 minutes

Calories per serving: 215

Freezing: not recommended

Wholesome, flaky fish topped with breadcrumbs, spices and herbs makes a winning combination.

low fat cooking spray
½ small onion, diced
½ teaspoon ground cumin
2 tablespoons chopped fresh coriander
50 g (1¾ oz) fresh white breadcrumbs
2 × 150 g (5½ oz) cod fillets
salt and freshly ground black pepper
200 g (7 oz) green beans, to serve

1 Heat the low fat cooking spray in a small frying pan that can be put under the grill and sauté the onion for 4–5 minutes, until starting to soften.

2 Add the ground cumin, mix well and cook for 1 minute.

3 Place the coriander and fresh breadcrumbs in a bowl and then add the spicy onion mixture. Mix together well.

4 Place the cod fillets on a piece of kitchen paper and season well. Using your hands, divide the breadcrumb mixture between the two cod fillets, squeezing it to make it into a paste and patting it down on to the top of the fish.

5 Preheat the grill to high.

6 Spray the frying pan with low fat cooking spray again and place the cod fillets crust side up in the pan.

Cook for 8–10 minutes until starting to turn golden underneath.

7 Place the pan under the grill and cook for another 6–8 minutes, until the top is golden and crispy.

8 Meanwhile, cook the green beans in lightly salted boiling water for 4–5 minutes. Drain well and season to taste.

9 Serve the cod with green beans.

Variation Most flaky fish can be used for this recipe. You can also vary the spices and herbs. Try salmon with a little mustard powder and fresh dill. The Points per serving will then be 5½.

SEARED TUNA WITH MEXICAN SALSA

4½ POINTS

9 Points per recipe

Serves 2

Preparation time: 15 minutes

Cooking time: 20 minutes

Calories per serving: 260

Freezing: not recommended

A simple but great tasting recipe – chunky fish with a spicy salsa. Serve with steamed No Point vegetables, such as mange tout or baby corn.

low fat cooking spray
2 × 100 g (3½ oz) tuna steaks
For the salsa
½ red onion, diced
3 plum tomatoes, diced
1 avocado, diced
grated zest and juice of ½ lime
a few drops of Tabasco sauce
freshly ground black pepper

1 Mix together the diced red onion, tomatoes and avocado, and then mix in the lime juice and zest. Add the Tabasco sauce and season with freshly ground black pepper. Cover and leave at room temperature.

2 Heat a frying pan, spray with low fat cooking spray and add the tuna. Cook for about 10 minutes on one side and then turn over and cook for the same time on the other.

3 Serve the tuna with the salsa.

Top tip Tuna is cooked when it changes from dark pink to a light, opaque pink – try not to overcook it as this will make it tough.

Seared Tuna with Mexican Salsa: Spice up your tuna the Mexican way for 4½ Points per serving.

KING PRAWN KEBABS

3 Points per recipe

Serves 4

Preparation time: 5 minutes +
marinating

Cooking time: 8–10 minutes

Calories per serving: 95

Freezing: not recommended

Great for a barbecue or summer lunch, these prawn kebabs are marinated in honey and spicy hoisin sauce.

| 200 g (7 oz) raw king prawns |
| 1 medium courgette, sliced |
| 1 red pepper, de-seeded and cut into chunks |
| lettuce leaves, to serve |
| **For the marinade** |
| 2 tablespoons soy sauce |
| 1/2 tablespoon honey |
| 1 tablespoon hoisin sauce |
| 1 garlic clove, crushed |
| 1 teaspoon lemon juice |

1 Place the prawns in a glass bowl or plastic container. Mix together the marinade ingredients.

2 Pour the marinade over the prawns and mix well before covering and placing in the fridge for at least 1 hour. Soak 8 wooden kebab skewers in plenty of water for at least 30 minutes to prevent them from burning.

3 Thread the prawns, courgette slices and pieces of red pepper on to the kebab sticks and cook under a hot grill or on the barbecue until the prawns turn pink, turning over once. Baste with the marinade while cooking.

4 Serve on a bed of crisp lettuce.

CAJUN COD

1 Point per recipe

Serves 1

Preparation time: 8 minutes

Cooking time: 12–15 minutes

Calories per serving: 160

Freezing: not recommended

A quick meal for one – a fillet of cod cooked with Cajun spices on a bed of tomatoes and okra. Cajun recipes normally call for catfish, but cod tastes just as good!

| low fat cooking spray |
| 1/2 onion, chopped |
| 227 g (8 oz) canned chopped tomatoes |
| 50 g (1 3/4 oz) okra |
| 90 g (3 1/4 oz) cod fillet |
| 2 teaspoons Cajun Spice |
| salt and freshly ground black pepper |

1 Heat a small pan and spray with low fat cooking spray. Cook the onion for 3–4 minutes, until starting to soften.

2 Pour in the tomatoes and add the okra. Season well and then simmer for 8–10 minutes until the okra is cooked.

3 Meanwhile wash the cod fillet and dry with kitchen paper. Sprinkle with the Cajun spice, patting it all over the fish.

4 Heat a small pan and spray with low fat cooking spray. Cook the fish, skin side down, for 6–7 minutes until the skin starts to blacken. Turn over and cook for another 4–5 minutes and then serve on top of the tomatoes and okra.

Variation Salmon is also delicious cooked this way. Use a 110 g (4 oz) salmon fillet and the Points will be 3 1/2 per serving.

SQUID IN SPICY SPINACH SAUCE

15 1/2 Points per recipe:

Serves 4

Preparation time: 10 minutes

Cooking time: 15 minutes

Calories per serving: 335

Freezing: not recommended

An unusual but delicious way to serve squid, with lots of lovely spices, and a creamy spinach sauce.

| low fat cooking spray |
| 1/2 onion, chopped finely |
| 2 garlic cloves, chopped finely |
| 1 cm (1/2 inch) piece of fresh root ginger, peeled and grated |
| 1/2 teaspoon ground cumin |
| 1/2 teaspoon ground coriander |
| 1/2 teaspoon turmeric |
| 1/4 teaspoon chilli powder |
| 2 tomatoes, chopped |
| 200 g (7 oz) frozen spinach, defrosted |
| 250 g (9 oz) egg noodles |
| 300 g (10 1/2 oz) fresh squid, cut into strips |
| salt and freshly ground black pepper |

1 Heat a frying pan and spray with low fat cooking spray. Add the onion, garlic and ginger and stir-fry for 3–4 minutes.

2 Add the spices and stir well before adding the tomatoes and spinach. Stir well and pour in 200 ml (7 fl oz) of water. Bring to a simmer and cook for 4–5 minutes.

3 Meanwhile, in a saucepan cook the egg noodles according to the packet instructions. Drain well.

4 Add the squid and simmer for another 4–5 minutes until the squid is cooked. Check the seasoning and serve with egg noodles.

FISH STEW WITH SAFFRON

1½ POINTS

8½ Points per recipe

Serves 6
Preparation time: 15 minutes
Cooking time: 12 minutes
Calories per serving: 125
Freezing: not recommended

A wholesome, tasty fish dish. Serve with a medium crusty brown roll to soak up the juices – but don't forget to add 2 extra Points!

low fat cooking spray
3 shallots, chopped
1 leek, sliced
2 carrots, diced
2 celery sticks, diced
400 g (14 oz) canned chopped tomatoes
a pinch of saffron threads
600 ml (1 pint) hot fish stock
400 g (14 oz) cod, cut into bite size pieces
200 g (7 oz) raw prawns
salt and freshly ground black pepper
a bunch of fresh parsley, chopped

1 Spray a medium pan with low fat cooking spray and add the shallots, leek, carrots and celery. Stir fry for 3–4 minutes until starting to soften.

2 Add the chopped tomatoes and cook for another 2–3 minutes.

3 Meanwhile, add the saffron threads to the hot fish stock and leave to infuse for 2 minutes.

4 Pour the saffron infused stock into the pan and add the cod and prawns.

5 Season and bring to a simmer. Simmer for 4–5 minutes until the prawns turn pink and the cod turns white.

6 Check the seasoning, stir in the chopped parsley and serve.

Fish Stew with Saffron: A wonderful winter warmer for 1½ Points per serving.

cooling
desserts

From creamy and cooling to exotic and spicy, this chapter is filled with a wonderful selection of low Point desserts and bakes that are perfect to follow a spicy meal. All the desserts are quick and easy to make, but look so impressive and taste fantastic.

HOT PEPPERED PINEAPPLE

6½ Points per recipe

Serves 4

Preparation time: 15 minutes

Cooking time: 15 minutes +

30 minutes cooling time

Calories per serving: 70

Freezing: not recommended

A deliciously different recipe – pineapple that is blanched with pepper and sugar syrup and then griddled and topped with creamy crème fraiche.

---

1 medium pineapple, peeled, cored and cut into thick half moon slices

300 ml (½ pint) water

2 teaspoons artificial sweetener

¼ teaspoon freshly ground black pepper

75 g (2¾ oz) half fat crème fraîche

---

1 Place the pineapple slices in a medium saucepan with the water, sweetener and pepper. Bring to the boil and then simmer for 8–10 minutes until the pineapple is tender but not too soft.

2 Take the pan off the heat and leave the pineapple to cool in the syrup

3 Heat a griddle pan until it is really hot and place the pineapple slices on it. Cook on both sides, briefly – just enough to colour and slightly char them.

4 Serve the pineapple with the low fat crème fraîche.

Top tip If you find that the pineapple is too hot, add slightly less pepper next time.

Hot Peppered
Pineapple:
Pineapple with
a twist for
1½ Points
per serving.

**Baked Alaska:
Great for a
special occasion
for only 3 Points
per serving.**

BAKED ALASKA

12 Points per recipe

Ⓥ Serves 4

Preparation time: 10 minutes

Cooking time: 8–10 minutes

Calories per serving: 150

Freezing: not recommended

A very impressive and delicious dessert for a dinner party. It looks fantastic and is one of the easiest puddings to make.

1 medium (75 g/2³/₄ oz) sponge flan case

400 ml (14 fl oz) low fat vanilla ice cream

3 egg whites

3 tablespoons sugar

1 Preheat the oven to Gas Mark 8/ 230°C/fan oven 210°C.

2 Place the sponge flan case on a baking tray.

3 In a clean bowl, whisk the egg whites until stiff then gradually add the sugar and keep whisking until you have a stiff, glossy mixture.

4 Quickly spoon the ice cream into the flan case and press into a rounded shape.

5 Cover the whole flan case and ice cream with meringue and make a pattern of little peaks by patting the meringue with the back of a spoon.

6 Place in the oven and cook for 8–10 minutes until golden. Keep a close eye on this as it will change from golden to black very quickly!

7 Serve immediately.

Top tip When whisking egg whites, the bowl must always be completely grease free or the whites will not stiffen.

CARDAMOM RICE PUDDING

10 Points per recipe

Ⓥ Serves 4

Preparation time: 5 minutes

Cooking time: 20 minutes

Calories per serving: 195

Freezing: not recommended

A slight twist on traditional rice pudding – with a lovely hint of spice and dried fruit.

600 ml (1 pint) skimmed milk

100 g (3¹/₂ oz) basmati rice

5 cardamom pods, crushed and husks discarded

75 g (2³/₄ oz) sultanas

1 teaspoon artificial sweetener

a pinch of ground nutmeg

1 Pour the milk into a medium pan and add the rice and cardamom seeds.

2 Bring to the boil and then simmer gently for 18–20 minutes, stirring occasionally, until nearly all the milk has been absorbed.

3 Add the sultanas and sweetener and continue to simmer and stir until the pudding is really creamy but not too thick.

4 Serve warm, sprinkled with nutmeg.

Variation If you don't have sultanas try using the same amount of chopped prunes or apricots instead. The Points will then be reduced to 2 per serving.

CUMIN SHORTBREAD

20 Points per recipe

 Makes 8 pieces

*Preparation time: 12 minutes +
10 minutes chilling time
Cooking time: 40 minutes
Calories per piece: 145
Freezing: recommended for up to
1 month*

Light, spicy shortbread, ideal after
a light meal or with afternoon tea!

---

110 g (4 oz) low fat spread

50 g (1³/4 oz) caster sugar

120 g (4¹/4 oz) plain flour

40 g (1¹/2 oz) rice flour or cornflour

¹/2 teaspoon ground cumin

---

1 Preheat the oven to Gas Mark 4/
180°C/fan oven 160°C.

2 Beat the low fat spread in a bowl
to soften.

3 Add the sugar to the low fat spread
and beat together. Sift in the flours
and cumin and mix to a dough with
a wooden spoon.

4 Wrap the dough in cling film and
chill for 10 minutes.

5 Press the shortbread dough into
a circle measuring approximately
20 cm (8 inches) on a baking sheet.
Decorate the edges with a fork and
gently mark eight wedges out with
a knife.

6 Bake for 40 minutes until golden.
Remove from the oven and leave
to cool slightly before placing on a
cooling rack.

Variation For ginger shortbread,
replace the ground cumin with
ground ginger. The Points will
remain the same.

Top tip You can buy rice flour in
health food shops.

YOGURT PUDDING

14 Points per recipe

 Serves 4

*Preparation time: 15 minutes
Cooking time: 40 minutes
Calories per serving: 250
Freezing: not recommended*

This is a great pudding – when
baked it develops a light cake like
texture on the top and lemony egg
custard underneath – delicious!

---

3 eggs, separated

75 g (2³/4 oz) caster sugar

1 vanilla pod

---

25 g (1 oz) plain flour

grated zest of ¹/2 orange

grated zest of 1 lemon

350 g (12 oz) plain low fat yogurt

*25 g (1 oz) shelled pistachio nuts,
roughly chopped*

---

1 Preheat the oven to Gas Mark 4/
180°C/fan oven 160°C.

2 Place the egg yolks in a bowl and
beat with 60 g (2 oz) of the caster
sugar until pale.

3 Slit the vanilla pod and scrape
out the seeds. Add these to the egg
mixture along with the flour, orange
and lemon zest and low fat yogurt.
Mix well.

4 Whisk the egg whites until stiff and
then whisk in the remaining sugar.

5 Gently fold the egg whites into
the yogurt mixture and then pour
into a baking tin or dish measuring
20 × 20 cm (8 × 8 inches).

6 Sprinkle over the pistachio nuts
and place the baking tin or dish in a
roasting tray. Pour hot water into the
roasting tray, to come about half way
up the baking dish. Place in the
preheated oven and cook for 40
minutes.

7 Serve hot or cold.

Cumin Shortbread:
Add a hint of spice
to teatime for 2½
Points per slice.

Mint Kulfi: Creamy and delicious – for only 2 Points per serving!

MINT KULFI

16½ Points per recipe

(V) *Serves 8*

Preparation time: 20 minutes +
freezing

Calories per serving: 180

Freezing: recommended

Kulfi is a rich and creamy Indian
ice cream – great for those special
occasions.

400 ml (14 fl oz) skimmed milk
397 g can of condensed milk
½ teaspoon mint flavouring

1 Pour the skimmed milk into a
medium non stick pan and slowly
bring to a simmer.

2 Add the condensed milk and
bring back to a simmer, stirring
constantly. Continue to stir and
simmer for 10–12 minutes – the
mixture will thicken very slightly.

3 Add the mint flavouring and stir
for a couple more minutes.

4 Pour the custard into eight dariole
moulds (or similar cone shape
moulds that can be frozen) and
leave to cool.

5 When cool enough, cover with
cling film or foil and place in the
freezer for 6–7 hours, or overnight.

6 To serve, remove from the freezer
and dip into a bowl of warm water
and then tip out on to a plate or
shallow dish and serve.

Variations For mango kulfi, purée
1 mango and add to the mixture,
instead of the mint, before cooling.
The Points per serving will be 2½.
Half a teaspoon of menthol liqueur
could be used instead of mint
flavouring. The Points per serving
will remain the same.

RUSSIAN CHEESECAKE

14 Points per recipe

(V) *Serves 10*

Preparation time: 15 minutes +
6 hours chilling

Calories per serving: 95

Freezing: not recommended

A delicious Russian cheesecake,
called Pashka, is produced as a
special treat at Easter (Pashka in
Russian means Easter). This is a
simple low Point version – but is
absolutely delicious!

300 g (10½ oz) quark
50 g (1¾ oz) low fat spread
1 egg yolk
½ teaspoon vanilla essence
1 tablespoon caster sugar
25 g (1 oz) flaked almonds, toasted
100 g (3½ oz) dried apricots, chopped
grated zest of ½ lemon

1 Line an 18 cm (7 inch) loose
bottomed tin with greaseproof paper.
Place the quark in a food processor
or blender and blend until smooth.

2 Add the low fat spread, egg yolk
and vanilla essence and blend until
they are mixed together.

3 Stir in the sugar, flaked almonds,
dried apricots and grated lemon zest.

4 Pour the mixture into the prepared
tin, cover with cling film and place
in the fridge for at least 6 hours,
preferably overnight.

5 To remove from the tin, take off
the cling film and turn the tin over
on to a plate. Push the bottom of the
tin down to release the ring of the
tin. Remove the bottom and peel
off the greaseproof paper. Cut into
wedges and serve.

Variation Instead of dried apricots,
try dried pears, mango or figs. The
Points per serving remain the same.

Mango Fool: Creamy and fruity for only 2½ Points per serving.

MANGO FOOL

10 Points per recipe

Serves 4

Preparation time: 5 minutes

Calories per serving: 150

Freezing: not recommended

---

2 ripe mangoes

100 g (3¹/₂ oz) low fat crème fraiche

90 g (3¹/₄ oz) low fat plain yogurt

8 wafer thin biscuits, to serve

---

1 Peel the mangoes and cut off the flesh from the stone. Place half the fruit in a food processor and blend until smooth. Chop the remaining fruit and divide between four ramekins.

2 Beat together the crème fraiche and yogurt and stir in the pureed mango.

3 Pour the creamy mango mixture over the chopped mango and chill until ready to serve. Serve with the wafer thin biscuits, for dipping.

APRICOT AND LIME SORBET

1¹/₂ Points per recipe

Ⓥ Ⓥ̄ *Serves 4*

Preparation time: 30 minutes +
5 hours freezing time

Calories per serving: 25

Freezing: recommended

A refreshing dessert on a hot day!

---

325 g (11¹/₂ oz) fresh ripe apricots, halved and stones removed

3 tablespoons sweetener

juice of ¹/₂ lime

---

1 Place the apricots in a medium pan with 400 ml (14 fl oz) water and the sweetener. Bring to a simmer and cook for 20–25 minutes until soft.

2 Leave to cool and then place in a food processor or blender and blend until completely smooth.

3 Add the lime juice and check for sweetness – more sweetener or lime juice may be added according to your taste.

4 Place in a plastic sealed container and chill in the freezer. After 2 hours, whisk the mixture around with a fork, to break up the ice crystals. Repeat this again after 4 hours.

5 After 5 hours the sorbet should be ready to serve – frozen but still quite soft.

Top tip If you forget to whisk the sorbet or it freezes too hard, just break it up and blend in the food processor to break the ice crystals down again.

Apricot and Lime Sorbet: Deliciously tangy for only ¹/₂ a Point per serving.